GREG ERHABOR

THE POWER
OF JOY

HOW TO BE JOYFUL 24 HOURS OF THE
DAY AND 365⁺ DAYS OF THE YEAR

THE POWER OF JOY

Copyright
© Rev. Prof. G. E. Erhabor, 2010.

ISBN 1518668518

Unless otherwise stated, all scriptures are taken from
the **New King James Version** of the Bible.

Published by Spokesman Communication Ministries,
P.O. Box 1154, Ile-Ife, Nigeria.

Printed in Nigeria

ACKNOWLEDGEMENT

I am grateful to God and His blessed Spirit for inspiration and grace in fulfilling the mandate He has given me and in writing this book.

My sincere appreciation goes to my writing and research team for their relentless efforts in producing this book.

I am greatly indebted to my wonderful wife, Ayodele who has prayed for, encouraged and supported me in the work of the ministry; and to my children who believe in me and cheer me on. You are the best!

ACKNOWLEDGEMENT

CONTENTS

PREFACE

T he Psalmist wrote, "You will show me the path of life; in Your presence is fullness of joy; at Your right hand are pleasures forevermore" **(Psalm 16:11 NKJV).** Joy is always an expression of our relationship with God. The closer we are to God, the more joyful we are. Someone once said, "Joy is the flag flown high from the castle of my heart, when the King is in residence there."

Jesus told his apostles that they will experience problems, persecutions and perils in this life but they are commanded to maintain a joyful spirit. Paul admonished us to "Rejoice evermore" **(1 Thessalonians 5:16).** In this present world full of stress, we can still experience joy. Joy is not a product of chance like happiness but an expression of the life of God in us.

My prayer is that this book will help rekindle joy in your life, home, church and through you to the larger society. We can, like Prophet Habakkuk, say, "Although the fig tree shall not blossom, neither shall fruit be in the vines; the labour of the olive shall fail, and the fields shall yield no meat; the flock shall be cut off from the fold, and there shall be no herd in the stalls: Yet I will rejoice in the LORD, I will joy in the God of my salvation" **(Habakkuk 3:17-18).** And like the psalmist, we can declare, "Weeping may endure for a night, but joy cometh in the morning **(Psalm 30:5).**

May this book help you make joy, not just a transient phenomena but a lifestyle.

Rev. Prof. Greg Erhabor

O N E

WHAT IS JOY?

"But let all those rejoice who put their trust in You;
Let them ever shout for joy, because You defend
them; Let those also who love Your name be joyful
in You"
Psalm 5:11 NKJV.

Joy is a spiritual sense of internal equilibrium and well being. It is a state of perpetual rejoicing that springs from within. The word joy or joyful appeared in the scriptures two hundred and fifty times. And the word 'rejoice' appeared about two hundred times. In all, words pertaining to joy, joyful or rejoice occurred about four hundred and fifty times in the Bible. This shows the importance of joy in the heart of God. Like C. S. Lewis, renowned nineteenth century Christian scholar, who wrote 'Mere Christianity,' said, "Joy is the serious business of heaven." So if we are citizens of heaven, we should also demonstrate joy.

To rejoice means to be joyful, to express feelings of exceeding gladness and joy. Joy is **JOY IS A SPIRITUAL SENSE OF INTERNAL EQUILIBRIUM AND WELL-BEING.** more than positive mental attitude or psychological pep talk; its origin is embedded in God's nature. Our God is a God of joy. He gives joy and commands joy. Joy is an expression of faith in God, a confident assurance of His providence in all circumstances of life. It is an inner equanimity untouched by external dilemmas; it is neither marred by pain nor diminished by sorrow.

In the book 'Something Beautiful for God' by Malcolm Muggeridge, Mother Teresa, the world renowned missionary, humanitarian and recipient of the 1979 Nobel Peace Prize was quoted: "Joy is prayer, joy is strength, joy is love; joy is a net of love by which you can catch souls. God loves a cheerful giver. She gives most who gives with joy. The best way to show our gratitude to God and the people is to accept everything with joy. A joyful heart is the normal result of a heart burning with love. Never let anything fill you with sorrow as to make you forget the joy of the Risen Christ. We all long for heaven where God is but we can have it in our power to be with Him right now; to be happy with him at this very moment."

JOY IS MORE THAN POSITIVE MENTAL ATTITUDE OR PSYCHOLO- GICAL PEP TALK; ITS ORIGIN IS EMBEDDED IN GOD'S NATURE.

JOY IS THE SIGNATURE OF THE CHRISTIAN FAITH

"But when the high priests and the scribes saw the amazing things that he had done and the children shouting in the temple, "Hosanna to the Son of David," they became furious and asked him, "Do you hear what these people are saying?" Jesus said to them, "Yes! Haven't you ever read, 'From the mouths of infants and nursing babies you have created praise'?" (Matthew 21:15-16 ISV)

One of the things we find in this revival is the Joy that these children exemplify: "Hosanna to the Son of David." When Jesus steps into a life, He makes that life joyful. Joy bears the seal of Christ's presence in any life. One of the greatest moves this generation has had is the spread of the Full Gospel Businessmen. The founder wrote a book titled 'The Happiest People on Earth.' This is the Christian testimony. One of the amazing experiences newly converted Christians testify of is a profound unexplainable joy that wells from deep within.

JOY BEARS THE SEAL OF CHRIST'S PRESENCE IN ANY LIFE.

It is not something anybody can contest. You may not say that the children of God are the most influential on earth. You may never say that they are the richest on earth. But it is a fact that these are the happiest people on earth. If you come to a bank where a Christian is the manager, you will see the joy in his heart. If you visit a clinic where the Consulting doctor is a Christian, you will see the joy in him. If you come to a school where the teacher is a Christian, the first thing you will notice is the radiating joy. If you come to a home where Christians dwell, the first thing you will notice is the spontaneity of their joy. "Joy is the infallible sign of the Presence of God" *(Rev. Joyce)*.

C. S. Lewis shared the common misconception he had about the Christian life in his book 'Surprised by Joy.' After trying to evade God for a long time, he finally surrendered. He wrote, "In 1929, I gave in and admitted that God was God and knelt and prayed; perhaps that night, the most dejected and reluctant convert in all England." To his utmost surprise, he discovered that surrendering to Christ

SURRENDER-ING TO CHRIST IS NOT TO BE DEPRIVED OF JOY BUT TO BE FILLED TO OVERFLOWING BY IT. is not to be deprived of joy but to be filled to overflowing by it. He experienced great intense joy. Apostle Peter eloquently described the Christian joy,

> **"Though now you do not see Him, yet believing, you rejoice with joy inexpressible and full of glory"** (1 Peter 1:8 NKJV).

The Bible in Basic English decribes it as

> **"... Joy greater than words and full of glory."**

And Good News Bible says,

> **"...A great and glorious joy which words cannot express."**

Joy is synonymous with Christianity; it characterizes our faith. The well of joy springs from deep within and it never runs dry because Christ is the source. The Christian possesses joy that no one can take away. Many people do not associate God with joy; they think He frowns when we laugh or hates anything that does not involve sobriety. However, God is the first advocate of joy. A woman who got converted said in wonder, "Strange, but I never associated joy with God before." Why do many think that becoming a Christian is equivalent to giving up joy and the enjoyable things of life? God is not a killjoy; He wants us to abound with joy. Joy strengthens us and brings sunshine on rainy days. It is the silver lining our dark clouds; the wind beneath our wings. And God want us to revel in it.

GOD COMMANDS JOY

The Bible says in **Philippians 4:4,**

> **"Rejoice in the Lord always: and again I say, Rejoice."**

And the Psalmist intoned,

> **"Rejoice in the LORD, O ye righteous: for praise is comely for the upright" (Psalm 33:1).**

God does not just repeat His words. He emphasizes them because they are important so that by reading them over and over, we will know that joy should be part of the Christian life.

The Moffat's translation of **1 Thessalonians 5:16** says,

"Rejoice at all times."

The Christian joy is not once in a while; it is not to be engaged in when the situation is favourable; it should be 'at all times.' It is God's desire that we are joyful and He gives it as a command to us. John Wesley, the founder of Methodism speaking on Joy and Faith in his compilation 'The John Wesley Reader' said, "Christian joy is joy in obedience; joy in loving God and keeping His commandments …We rejoice in knowing that 'being justified through his grace, we have not received that grace of God in vain;' that God having freely …reconciled us to Himself, we run in the strength which he has given us, through the way of His commandments."

The more we obey the command of God to be joyful, the more we fully experience His presence on a daily basis. And the more we enjoy this presence, the easier it is to express and share joy. God wants us to bubble with joy, to radiate joy, to express joy and to encourage others with our joy. He wants us to bring His joy to our lives, our relationships, our homes, our places of work, our society and the world at large.

The angel declared,

> **"...Behold, I bring you good tidings of great joy, which shall be to all people" (Luke 2:10 KJV).**

The Lord's decree of joy is for all people; all races and He channels it through us to humanity; to the whole world. A. W. Tozer, American preacher and author, wrote, "The Christian owes it to the world

YOU ARE GOD'S GIFT OF JOY TO THE WORLD.

to be supernaturally joyful." You are God's gift of joy to the world.

T W O

JOY: A GIFT OF THE SPIRIT

"Joy is the echo of God's life in us."
Abbot Coumba Marmion

JOY TO THE WORLD!

The coming of Jesus was the announcement of joy. The angel proclaimed,

"... Behold, I bring you good tidings of great joy, which shall be to all people" (Luke 2:10 KJV).

Isaac Watts, renowned songwriter wrote in 1719,

> Joy to the world! The Lord is come,
> Let earth receive her King,
> Let every heart prepare Him room,
> And heaven and nature sing.
>
> Joy to the world! The Saviour reigns,
> Let men their songs employ,
> While fields and floods, rocks, hills and plains,
> Repeat the sounding joy.

A KING STEPPED ON THE EARTH WITH JOY ON HIS TRAIN. HE HERALDS JOY, HE PROCLAIMS JOY AND HE GIVES JOY.

A King stepped on the earth with joy on his train. He heralds joy, He proclaims joy and He gives joy. The tribulations and perplexities of life is such that removes joy from lives. But God does not desire a world of gloom; so He sent joy to the world through His Son. In **Jeremiah 31:13**, He declared:

"Then shall the virgin rejoice in the dance, both young men and old together: for I will

turn their mourning into joy, and will comfort them, and make them rejoice from their sorrow."

Christ came to restore joy to the world. The world system cannot proffer the solution for joy; it can only give sporadic periods of happiness, but in Christ we have unfailing joy. Jesus told the disciples,

"I have spoken these things to you so that you might have peace in me. In the world you shall have tribulation, but be of good cheer. I have overcome the world" (John 16:33 MKJV).

JOY IS A GIFT

Joy is an endowment not an attainment; it is what you obtain from God, not what you attain to. Joy is a product of the Spirit of God in you. The Pharisees could not experience joy, like the little children, because they were

JOY IS AN ENDOWMENT NOT AN ATTAINMENT; IT IS WHAT YOU OBTAIN FROM GOD, NOT WHAT YOU ATTAIN TO.

practicing religion, not having a relationship with God. To them, religion was a form of activity; there was no intimacy with God. God was something they practice outside; not someone they possess within. So, they could not understand the spontaneity of those little children. The world will not understand the spontaneity of your joy.

> JOY IS A MEANINGFUL ACCELERATION IN THE RHYTHM OF OUR RELATIONSHIP AND OUR UNDERSTANDING OF GOD.
> - EARL PALMER

Earl Palmer, a Presbyterian Minister and author, in his message 'The Search for Joy said, "Joy is a meaningful acceleration in the rhythm of our relationship and our understanding of God... Joy is a surprise gift. It's an experience of meaningful rhythmic acceleration. That's why there are strong feelings that go with joy. It's exuberant sometimes, but also profoundly quiet and peaceful. Notice they're both together. Also, joy is a surprise gift given to us and in us as a taste of the experience we have with the character of God... it's a taste of what celestial experience will be like. It's an advance look of what heaven will be like. Joy, in other words, is an experience of God's character. And then, evil cannot understand joy. It's a baffling experience to evil. It's opaque... It's baffling to evil and evil cannot stop it."

Galatians 5:22 tells us,

> **"But the fruit of the Spirit is love, joy, peace, longsuffering, gentleness, goodness, faith." KJV**

The Weymouth New Testament translates:

> **"The Spirit, on the other hand, brings a harvest of love, joy, peace; patience towards others, kindness, benevolence."**

And Good News Bible says:

> **"But the Spirit produces love, joy, peace, patience, kindness, goodness, faithfulness."**

Simply put, 'what the spirit of God manufactures in you, when you receive the seal of the Holy Ghost, is

"JOY IS THE FLAG FLOWN HIGH FROM THE CASTLE OF MY HEART, WHEN THE KING IS RESIDENT THERE."

joy.' The evidence that the Holy Ghost is in you is that you have love and joy. A songwriter wrote: "Joy is the flag flown high from the castle of my heart, when the King is resident there. So let it fly in the sky; let the whole world know, that the King is in residence here." When generals come into a city or arrive at an occasion, the insignia of presence is usually the flag. Whenever there is a flag, you know that the general is seated in the car. So, joy is the flag that every Christian bears when the Most High King is resident in his heart. When the Holy Ghost is in you, He demonstrates His presence with joy. **John 15:11** says,

> **"These things have I spoken unto you, that my joy might remain in you, and that your joy**

might be full." (King James Version)

"I have told you this so that my joy may be in you and that your joy may be complete." (New International Version)

"...That your joy may become perfect." (Weymouth New Testament)

"...That my joy may be felt in you." (Norton)

"...That you may share my joy." (Phillips)

In the above verse, Jesus was using a term that the people of the world would not understand. He says, 'My joy; what I possess.' If He says 'My joy,' it means there is another kind of joy that is different. He said 'I've spoken these things to you that my joy may be in you.' Simply put: 'that my joy might fill you up.' Whatsoever is happening around you, whatsoever challenges you're going through, my (Jesus) joy will fill you up and this joy will remain in you.

Paul told the Roman church:

"For the kingdom of God is not meat and drink; but righteousness, and peace, and joy in the Holy Ghost" (Romans 14:17 KJV).

This is in contrast with what we have in modern day Christianity; when someone tells you that the evidence of Christianity is that he has a big car, a big house or a fat bank account. Those are very terrestrial things; they have nothing to do with the essence of our relationship with God. Paul said, 'It is neither the car you have, nor the meat on your table, that determines God's presence. The evidence that He is with you is righteousness, peace and joy in the Holy Ghost.'

JOY CANNOT BE BOUGHT; IT CANNOT BE BORROWED, AND IT CANNOT BE BURIED.

This is what the world cannot buy. Joy cannot be bought; it cannot be borrowed, and it cannot be buried. In **Isaiah 35:10**, Prophet Isaiah declared,

"And the ransomed of the LORD shall return, and come to Zion with songs and everlasting

joy upon their heads: they shall obtain joy and gladness, and sorrow and sighing shall flee away" (KJV).

The Message Bible version says:

"The people GOD has ransomed will come back on this road. They'll sing as they make their way home to Zion, unfading halos of joy encircling their heads, welcomed home with gifts of joy and gladness as all sorrows and sighs scurry into the night."

The joy God gives is everlasting; it is different from the transient ecstasy the world gives. Now, you may say, 'You don't even understand my own situation. My wife does not understand me at all. My parents are very tyrannical. I work with a very difficult boss.' But the Bible says, 'You are different. You have been redeemed by the Lord and everlasting joy is on your head.'

THE JOY GOD GIVES IS EVERLASTING.

Isaiah 61:3 prophesied concerning the Saviour,

> "To appoint unto them that mourn in Zion, to give unto them beauty for ashes, the oil of joy for mourning, the garment of praise for the spirit of heaviness; that they might be called trees of righteousness, the planting of the LORD, that he might be glorified." KJV

God beautifies those who are in Zion. He gives them beauty for ashes, the oil of joy for the spirit of heaviness. Ashes signify a state when everything in your life has been destroyed; when almost all hope is gone. Your business is failing; things are not working the way they should. Everybody looks at you and tries to comfort you. Yet, at this period, God gives you a garment of joy for the spirit of heaviness.

THE JOY GOD GIVES CANNOT BE TAKEN AWAY

Joy is Spirit-given. And when God gives it, it cannot be taken away. Paul told the Romans:

"For the gifts and calling of God are without repentance" (Romans 11:29).

He does not recall or withdraw His gift of joy; it is permanent inside us. Much more than that, He preserves it so that no one can deprive us of that joy. **John 16:22** says,

> **"And ye now therefore have sorrow: but I will see you again, and your heart shall rejoice, and your joy no man taketh from you." KJV**

Let's look at some other translations:

> **"Therefore you now have sorrow, but I will see you again, and your heart will rejoice, and no one will take your joy away from you." WEB**

> **"...No one can rob you of your happiness." Williams**

> **"...And no one shall be able to deprive you of that joy." Berkeley**

"...And your joy shall no man snatch away from you." Montgomery

The Christian's joy is sheltered within the Lord's armour. While peace is tranquility within, joy is the bursting out of peace in the external. Dwight L. Moody, an eighteenth century American evangelist

WHILE PEACE IS TRANQUILITY WITHIN, JOY IS THE BURSTING OUT OF PEACE IN THE EXTERNAL.

recounted the story of a martyr who was brought before the King in the second century. "The king wanted him to recant and give up Christ but the man spurned the thought. The king said: "If you don't do it, I will banish you." The man smiled and answered: "You can't banish me from Christ. He says he will never leave me nor forsake me." The king got angry and said: "Well, I will confiscate your property and take it all from you." And the man replied: "My treasures are laid up on high; you cannot get them." The king became still more angry and said: "I will kill you." "Why," the man answered, "I have been dead forty years ago; I have been dead with Christ; dead to the world. My life is hid with Christ in God, and you cannot touch it." And so we can rejoice because we are resurrection ground, having risen with Christ. Let persecution and opposition come; your joy can no man take from you."

The Christian lives in the constant assurance that

"Weeping may endure for a night, but joy comes in the morning" (Psalm 30:5 NKJV).

We experience joy, even in the midst of persecutions and rejoice in the Lord when tribulations come. Sometimes ago, I had to take my son to the school before going to work. On the way, I noticed that something was smelling. I quickly tried to park the car but before we knew what was happening, the car was up in flames. A lot of vehicles quickly drove past; however some people stopped to help us. All through this incident, I

JOYFUL 'IN SPITE OF;' THAT IS THE REAL JOY, THE JOY THAT DERIVES ITS SOURCE FROM GOD'S BEING.

discovered that I was unperturbed. I was filled with the joy of the Holy Ghost and kept giving thanks for sparing our lives and sending help to us. I was joyful '*in spite of,*' that is the real joy, the joy that derives its source from God's being.

The story was told of Horatio Spafford, who wrote one of the most influential hymns in history, **"It is well with my Soul."** This hymn was written after several traumatic events in Spafford's life. The first was the death of his only son in 1871, shortly followed by the great Chicago Fire which ruined him financially (he had been a successful lawyer). Then in 1873, he had planned to travel to Europe with his family on the *SS Ville du Havre*, but sent the family ahead while he was delayed on business concerning zoning problems following the Great

Chicago Fire. While crossing the Atlantic, the ship sank after a collision with a sailing ship, and all four of Spafford's daughters died. His wife Anna survived and sent him the now famous telegram, "Saved alone." Shortly afterwards, as Spafford traveled to meet his grieving wife, he was inspired to write these words as his ship passed near where his daughters had died.

> When peace like a river, attendeth my way,
> When sorrows like sea billows roll,
> Whatever my lot, thou hast taught me to know,
> It is well, it is well with my soul.
>
> It is well, with my soul,
> It is well, with my soul,
> It is well, it is well with my soul,
>
> For me, be it Christ, be it Christ hence to live:
> If Jordan above me shall roll,
> No pang shall be mine, for in death as in life,
> Thou wilt whisper Thy peace to my soul.

Spafford exemplifies the Christian joy which endures in the midst of struggles and pain. Life's challenges cannot take our joy from us. When all else is lost, the joy of the Lord remains with us.

WHEN ALL ELSE IS LOST, THE JOY OF THE LORD REMAINS WITH US.

T H R E E

JOY IS NOT HAPPINESS

"Joy is not in things; it is in us."
Richard Wagner

oy includes happiness but it is not the same as happiness. The root meaning of the word happiness is derived from the English word '*happ*' which means 'chance.' We can also see its root in the Latin word '*fortuna*' which means 'luck.' So happiness, in a sense, is a chance thing; it is based on fortune. But joy transcends happiness because it's not dependent on something that has happened; it is perpetual.

> **JOY TRANSCENDS HAPPINESS BECAUSE IT'S NOT DEPENDENT ON SOMETHING THAT HAS HAPPENED; IT IS PERPETUAL.**

A joyful Christian is a happy Christian. But a happy person is not necessarily a joyful person. You can't say you are joyful but you are not happy. However, it is possible for you to be happy but you're not joyful. Let's look at a few differences between joy and happiness.

Happiness is always external; joy is always internal. Happiness is circumstantial; something happening around you but joy is something that is independent of circumstances. Happiness is always transient, but joy is something that is permanent. Happiness needs to be stimulated from outside; from promotion, from a stimulating drug; but joy is stirred up from within. Joy rises from within while happiness comes in from without.

Peter J. Kreeft, in his book 'Heaven the Heart's Deepest Longing' declared: "Joy seems to have a necessity to it, as God does... Joy itself is unchangeable, eternal and necessary. When it comes, though it appears new to us, a surprise, it also seems old, ancient, having existed 'before the beginning of time'... pleasure and happiness have nothing of that air of eternity about them that joy does." Happiness is limited to this life but joy is eternal. Happiness has a lot to do with your possessions but joy has to do with what possesses you. Happiness is the

HAPPINESS IS THE ABSENCE OF SADNESS BUT JOY CO-HABITS WITH SADNESS.

absence of sadness but joy co-habits with sadness. **2 Corinthians 6:10** says,

> **"As sorrowful, yet alway rejoicing; as poor, yet making many rich; as having nothing, and yet possessing all things."**

That is the paradox of our faith: sorrowful, yet rejoicing. In **2 Corinthians 7:4,** Paul says,

"Great is my boldness of speech toward you, great is my glorying of you: I am filled with comfort, I am exceeding joyful in all our tribulation."

He further declared in **2 Corinthians 4:8-9,**

"We are troubled on every side, yet not distressed; we are perplexed, but not in despair; Persecuted, but not forsaken; cast down, but not destroyed."

JOY IS 'IN SPITE OF,' NOT 'BECAUSE OF.' A person whose state of happiness is dependent on the present situations cannot make this declaration. Joy is *'in spite of,'* not *'because of.'* Joy is peace in the external. The Christian faith proffers joy in the midst of events which make people without faith unhappy. Robert Schuller, the Pastor of the Crystal Cathedral, Garden Grove, California wrote, "Joy is not the absence of suffering. It is the presence of God."

Happiness has to do with chance, but joy has to do

with choice. Someone once commented, "Joy springs from within; no one makes you joyous; you choose joyfulness." In as much as we **JOY IS PEACE IN THE EXTERNAL.** cannot create joy, we can choose to receive or reject the joy that the Lord has freely given us. We can decide to draw from the well of living waters deep within us. We can choose to obey God's command and live a life full of rejoicing.

There is a universal search for joy. However, man has made the pursuit of happiness the goal. He unfortunately looks for joy in the wrong places: advanced technology, material possessions, financial empowerment, seeking pleasure and transient euphoria in the form of sex, alcohol and wanton living. This has nonetheless led to more sorrows. Like C. S. Lewis said, "The modern man/woman has had an ever-increasing appetite for ever-decreasing pleasure." Joy can only be found in God.

God is the only one that has the signature for joy. Man can only sign your happiness. Whenever you see a man who is joyful, you know that God has put his ensign on him. God has put His mark. 'I bear the mark of the living God because the Bible says in His presence there is fullness of Joy.' The Psalmist says,

> "The voice of rejoicing and salvation is in the tabernacles of the righteous: the right hand of the LORD doeth valiantly" (Psalm 118:15 KJV).

Joy dwells in the tabernacle of the righteous. The joy of God cannot depart from our tabernacle; our tent, our temple. Paul asked in **1 Corinthians 3:16,**

> "Do you not know that you are the temple of God and that the Spirit of God dwells in you?"

And he boldly stated in **2 Corinthians 6:16,**

> "For you are the temple of the living God. As God has said: "I will dwell in them and walk among them. I will be their God, and they shall be My people."

God dwells inside us, we are his temple; therefore joy continually resides in us. Joy and happiness are not the same. However, you cannot be joyful and say you are not happy. Many people think that they get more joy when they add more to their lives. The pursuit of happiness is the beginning of sorrow. Why is this so? Man is dichotomous. He is a spiritual and a physical being. What sustains our joy is the spiritual. There is a seat of joy inside us and only God can fill it. Some might say, I want to fill this emptiness with money, I want to fill it with cash or I want to fill it with gold. But the more they have of these things, the more joy eludes them. In his book, 'How to be a Winner and Influence Anybody,' James Merritt told the story of a customer who went to a restaurant.

> The well dressed customer was staring sullenly at his drink. The waitress, trying to be kind, asked if something was wrong. "Well, two months ago, my grandfather died and left me

$185,000 in oil wells."

"That doesn't sound like something to get upset about," the waitress replied.

"Yeah," said the young man, "but last month my uncle passed away and left me $100,000 in stocks."

"So why are you sitting there so unhappy?"

"Because this month, so far, nobody has left me a cent!"

The more he got, the happier he was but when nobody left him anything, he got sad. Money can never satisfy. It has been said that "Millionaires seldom smile." Sophisticated societies produce more miserable people. Material things can never be enough and when we base our happiness on such we will never be joyful.

The story was told of a judge who was trying to sentence a robber; the robber owned up to the crime. The judge said, "I notice in addition to stealing money, you also took diamonds, rings, and precious pearls." He replied, "Yes, sir, I have always been taught that money alone does not bring happiness." So after stealing the whole money he took diamonds, pearls, and rings, hoping that the more he takes, the happier he will get. There is a vacuum which God is supposed to fill in our heart. Wealth, connection and fame cannot fill this void. And if you don't deal with the issue of your soul and allow God fill the void that is there, you can never know the joy that Jesus gives. The Psalmist says in **Psalms 4:7,**

> **"God puts joy in my heart much more than when their corn and their wine multiply."**

The New Living Translation says,

> **"You have given me greater joy than those who have abundant harvests of grain and new wine."**

Psalms 16:11 says,

"Thou wilt shew me the path of life: in thy presence is fulness of joy; at thy right hand there are pleasures for evermore."

Somebody said, "Money really brings a lot of luxury but it makes you miserable in your luxury." Below is a brief summary of the differences between joy and happiness.

HAPPINESS DIFFERS FROM JOY

	Happiness is:	Joy is:
a.	External	Internal
b.	Circumstantial	Independent of circumstances
c.	Transient	Permanent
d.	Stimulant is from without	Stirred from within
e.	Based on your possessions	Based on what you possess within you
f.	Occurs in the absence of sadness	May cohabit with sadness
g.	By chance	By choice
h.	Man signs happiness	**God has the signature of joy**
i.	Terrestrial	Celestial

The Power of Internal Control

Are you a thermostat or a thermometer? Are you controlled from events outside you or you have developed self control within? The power to control yourself from within is central to maintaining a joyful life.

Regardless of where we are, we will face challenges that will affect our happiness and moods. However, the state of our inner being will determine our response. A joyful person is more like a thermostat that controls the environment while a happy person is like a thermometer whose moods fluctuates with the circumstances around.

THE POWER TO CONTROL YOURSELF FROM WITHIN IS CENTRAL TO MAINTAINING A JOYFUL LIFE.

Psychologists have written extensively on what is referred to as the 'Locus of Control.' The concept was developed originally by Julian Rotter in the

1950s. It refers to an individual's perception about the underlying main causes of events in his or her life. The concept says that our response to life and events is based on whether our locus of control is 'external' or 'internal.' Philip Zimbardo, a famous psychologist wrote: "A locus of control orientation is a belief about whether the outcomes of our actions are contingent on what we do (internal control orientation) or on events outside our personal control (external control orientation)."

External locus of control is when the power controlling your happiness is outside you. The key to your emotional control, actions, decision making process, response ability and relational capacity is tied to events around you and you are being held bound by these circumstances.

EXTERNAL LOCUS OF CONTROL IS WHEN THE POWER CONTROLLING YOUR HAPPINESS IS OUTSIDE YOU.

You have external control to the degree to which you have little or no control over the affairs of your life. As it were, when the external factors are favourable, you are happy but when they are not, you feel a sense of despair; a sense of helplessness.

YOU HAVE EXTERNAL CONTROL TO THE DEGREE TO WHICH YOU HAVE LITTLE OR NO CONTROL OVER THE AFFAIRS OF YOUR LIFE.

The internal locus of control, on the other hand, is the ability to rely less on external factors to determine your emotional state or actions. You are more or less in charge, make personal and proactive decisions and take responsibility for your actions. This control derives its source from your inner being and is not affected by external turn of events. There is a feeling of being in control which induces passion, purposefulness and progress.

The degree to which you are controlled by the external or internal locus determines the extent to which you will be happy or joyful. To have joy, you

THE INTERNAL LOCUS OF CONTROL IS THE ABILITY TO RELY LESS ON EXTERNAL FACTORS TO DETERMINE YOUR EMOTIONAL STATE OR ACTIONS.

must develop an internal control which does not fluctuate with the turn of events.

I believe that to have an effective control from within, you have to recognize the power of God within. Jesus said,

"For, behold, the kingdom of God is within you" (Luke 17:21 KJV).

Romans 14:17 says,

"For the kingdom of God is not meat and drink; but righteousness, and peace, and joy in the Holy Ghost."

And Apostle Paul declared,

"...Christ in you, the hope of glory" (Colossians 1:27).

Internal control is dependent more on relationship with God and proactive personal decision to act positive and joyful in the face of varying circumstances.

We can maintain an internal equilibrium that can help us put things outside us, under God's control. Rather than being regulated by what is external, we have an internal thermostat that regulates our external to fit our

INTERNAL CONTROL IS DEPENDENT MORE ON RELATIONSHIP WITH GOD.

internal environment; which is full of righteousness, peace and joy in the Holy Ghost. Christ said,

> "Peace I leave with you, My peace I give to you; not as the world gives do I give to you. Let not your heart be troubled, neither let it be afraid" (John 14:27 NKJV).

It is this internal peace and joy that is demonstrated as we relate with people in our homes, workplace and the larger society. When we lack this internal control, we become victims of circumstances and fall prey to the whims and caprices of situations and people around us.

F O U R

HOW TO GET JOY - 1

"You have shown me the paths that lead to life,
And your presence will fill me with joy."
Act 2:28 GNB

PUT YOUR EXPECTATION IN GOD ALONE

"My soul, wait thou only upon God; for my expectation is from him" (Psalms 62:5 KJV).

God is the source of our total supply. He is the Ultimate and has the key to all our needs, both spiritual and physical. You can never get joy until you put your expectation only

PUTTING OUR TRUST IN MEN IS A GOOD RECIPE FOR SADNESS AND MISERY. in Him. Many people are miserable, because they have expected certain things from certain people. Maybe my husband will do this for me. Perhaps my wife will do that for me. Maybe the federal government will increase our pay packet. Perhaps somebody in this church will reach out to me. Putting our trust in men is a good recipe for sadness and misery. The psalmist was very clear; "My soul wait *only* on the Lord for my expectation is from Him." He went further to say,

> "Whom have I in heaven but thee? And there is none upon earth that I desire beside thee" (Psalm 73:25 KJV).

If you are going to maintain your joy, realize that men are instruments in the hands of God; do not turn them to gods. God is the Supreme noun, He is not an adjective. God is in charge. He's the ultimate;

He's the all-inclusive clause. He's the God of all things, including those who you are going to meet for help. **Proverbs 24:14** says,

> GOD IS THE SUPREME NOUN, HE IS NOT AN ADJECTIVE. HE'S THE ULTIMATE ... THE ALL-INCLUSIVE CLAUSE.

> **"So shall the knowledge of wisdom be unto thy soul: when thou hast found it, then there shall be a reward, and thy expectation shall not be cut off."**

SEE THE END OF IT ALL- THE JOY SET BEFORE YOU

> **"Looking to Jesus the author and finisher of our faith; who for the joy that was set before him endured the cross, despising the shame, and is set down at the right hand of the throne of God" (Hebrews 12:2 Webster).**

Many people are not joyful because their sole focus is on the now. One of the attributes of Jesus Christ was His ability to keep His view on the end. The

Hebrew writer tells us that Jesus, while He was on this earth kept on looking at the joy that was set before Him. The Message Bible says, "Simply fixing our gaze upon Jesus, our Prince Leader in the faith, who will also award us the prize. He, for the sake of the joy which lay before Him, patiently endured the cross, looking with contempt upon its shame, and afterwards seated Himself-- where He still sits--at the right hand of the throne of God."

There is a joy that is ahead of you. Whatsoever ministry or task God has given you, patiently pursue it. You may be a student studying for a degree, or an employee desiring a promotion; there is a joy that is ahead of you. However, the journey towards this joy requires endurance. That was what Jesus did. They spat at him, they abused him, they told lies against him; but Jesus kept on looking at the joy that was ahead of Him.

When we first started our church, we faced a lot of challenges. There were days when the place we used was so hot, periods when the chairs were not comfortable and the people were few; there were occasions when the finance was low but somehow in my spirit I knew the joy that was set before us. I knew that God wants us to have a very beautiful church that will be a testimony to His glory. Because of the joy ahead, I endured those pains and sufferings.

International Standard Version says,

"Who, in view of the joy set before him..."

Moffat's translation puts it this way:

"In order to reach his own appointed joy..."

You see there is an appointed joy for everyone. For every journey you are taking, there is an appointed joy; an appointed time and place. That is what makes a woman endure the pains of childbirth because she knows that there is an appointed joy ahead of her, the joy of having a baby.

John 16:21 says,

"A woman when she is in travail hath sorrow, because her hour is come: but as soon as she is delivered of the child, she remembereth no more the anguish, for joy that a man is born into the world."

And Prophet Isaiah wrote:

"Who hath heard such a thing? Who hath seen such things? Shall the earth be made to bring forth in one day? Or shall a nation be born at once? For as soon as Zion travailed, she brought forth her children" (Isaiah 66:8).

> ENDURE THE MOMENTARY SO YOU CAN ENJOY THE PERMANENT. ENJOY THE JOURNEY WHILE YOU FOCUS ON THE DESTINATION.

Endure the momentary so you can enjoy the permanent. Enjoy the journey while you focus on the destination. Endure the pains so that you can have the pleasure. Marianne Williamson, in her book, 'A Woman's Worth,' wrote, "Joy is what happens when we allow ourselves to recognize how good things are. Joy is not necessarily what happens when things unfold according to our plans." Paul told the Romans,

> **"Rejoicing in hope; patient in tribulation; continuing instant in prayer" (Romans 12:12 KJV).**

There is an appointed joy for you, just reach out for it. No matter what you are going through, just look at what is ahead of you. Never lose sight of where you are going. And look at Jesus who endured those contradictions of sinners upon himself because there is a joy that is appointed for Him.

EXAMINE YOURSELF

Something somewhere has stood between you and God; you need to find it and bring it before God. Many Christians lose their joy because they don't take time to examine themselves. The joy that you and I have is the joy of the Lord. And the joy of the Lord is based on relationship. Christianity is not what you do but who you are in terms of your

CHRISTIANITY IS NOT WHAT YOU DO BUT WHO YOU ARE IN TERMS OF YOUR RELATIONSHIP WITH GOD. relationship with God. Christianity is not about Do's and Don'ts, it is a relationship. You have to examine your life from time to time to determine your stand with God. Ask: How am I related to Jesus? What is standing between us?

It may just be a little thought, it may be a careless word; it may be misappropriated deeds. It may be what David referred to as secret sin. In **Psalm 19:14**, he said,

> **"Let the words of my mouth and the meditation of my heart be acceptable in your sight, O LORD, my strength and my Redeemer."**

Let my unspoken thoughts and my spoken words be acceptable to you. Whatsoever can stand as a gap between you and God will spoil your joy. When you see that you are not joyful as you should be, rather than blaming external things or people; examine yourself. If you judge yourself, then no one can judge you. Take time to look into the mirror of the Word of God, which reveals all stains and sins. Submerge yourself in the cleansing power of the blood and let it wash you from all iniquities.

SEEK EMANCIPATION FROM THE YOKE OF SIN AND SATAN

"If I regard iniquity in my heart, the Lord will not hear me" (Psalm 66:18).

Emancipation is the act or process of being set free from restrictions. In other words, when we seek emancipation we desire to be set free of yokes and bondages that put restrictions on our lives and steal our joy.

One of the things that can deprive us of joy is a hard heart. It is to have a very stubborn, rebellious heart; an unforgiving, unrepentant heart. My uncle has been cruel to me; I will never forgive him. My father has not treated me well; I will never respect him. The more you hold on to these grudges, the less joyful you become.

When we do not confront sin in our lives, we lose our joy but when we repent of sin, we experience deep wells of joy. Seek emancipation from every yoke of sin and bondage. Ask God for freedom from the bondage the enemy has put into your soul and spirit.

DON'T DEVELOP A REPUTATION FOR BEING A HARD PERSON. IT IS BETTER TO LOSE AN ARGUMENT BUT WIN A FRIEND.

Emancipation implies liberty, freedom, deliverance; to be set free. Set yourself free of the hold of sin, malice, and bitterness. Be free of the hold of stubbornness. When you know that these things will affect your relationship with God, then you must reconcile. Don't develop a reputation for being a hard person. It is better to lose an argument but win a friend. The

Bible says,

> **"It is better to dwell in the wilderness, than with a contentious and an angry woman" (Proverb 21:19).**

And **Proverb 15:17** says,

> **"Better is a dinner of herbs where love is, than a stalled ox and hatred therewith."**

It is better to be considered a fool but peaceful than to be considered a wise person full of strife. It is better to be looked down upon but quiet and joyful than for you to oppress other people but sad. I like this verse in the scriptures which says,

> **"Behold, how good and how pleasant it is for brethren to dwell together in unity!" (Psalm 133:1 KJV)**

When there is love, there is goodness; there is joy and pleasantness. But when there is discord and disharmony, there is unhappiness. It does not matter who you are, you would not be joyful. You may be a well dressed man, but you will be a well dressed miserable man. You may be an important CEO, but you're an important but bitter CEO. You may be a domineering husband whom everybody fears, but you'll be dying inside because you are not a joyful person.

What does it take to give yourself a spiritual lift? What would it cost to forgive and forget offences? If you decide to hold on to grudges, who gets hurt? Who is sad? Who is miserable? Who is bitter? Who is disorganized? Unfortunately, it is not the other party; you get to suffer more from the effects of bitterness. Unforgiveness is a sin that destroys the person that hold on to an offence, while enriching the one who committed the wrong. Why not free yourself? Why not ask God to remove anything that will hinder your fellowship with Him. Lose an argument but win a friend. Choose to be peaceful than to be a bitter man. I'll rather be somebody that nobody thinks about but joyful in God, than someone everybody honours yet miserable.

F I V E

HOW TO GET JOY - 2

"May your walls know joy; may every room hold
laughter and every window open to great
possibility."
Maryanne Radmacher-Hershey

JOY IS A CHOICE

Joy does not come by chance, it is a choice. It is not just an emotion but an attitude. In as much as God has given us the wellspring of joy when we got saved, we are still required to draw from this well on a regular basis. We have to choose to be joyful. The Psalmist declared:

"Light-seeds are planted in the souls of God's

> people; Joy-seeds are planted in good heart-soil. So, God's people, shout praise to GOD, Give thanks to our Holy God!" (Psalm 97:11-12 MSG)

The seeds of joy have been planted; let the people of God shout praise to Him. 'Shout' is an action word. It is what you do willingly; it is a choice. Despite the fact that the seeds have been planted, the people of God can choose not to express joy. They can decide to remain gloomy or... be joyful. The concept of choice in life's decision is what several people have not fully understood. Many have fallen victim of the 'defeatist' mentality in which they believe that whatever comes their way is their destiny and that they have no choice in the matter. Most of us grew up believing that our moods are supposed to be reflections of the circumstances around us, that we don't have control over our

JOY DOES NOT COME BY CHANCE, IT IS A CHOICE. IT IS NOT JUST AN EMOTION BUT AN ATTITUDE.

moods and emotion. However, the truth remains that you can choose your actions in every circumstance that life presents. You can choose a good mood, a joyous mood just by making a mental shift or you can choose a depressed mood. You can choose love, joy, peace, goodwill; you can choose your attitude.

Tim Hansel, the founder of Summit Expedition was a man who was well acquainted with chronic pain and suffering. During a mountaineering expedition, Tim fell into the crevasse where he landed on his neck, compressing several vertebrae and subsequently became unconscious. Tim regained consciousness; however, the following morning, he started having intense pain. His doctors announced the injury was inoperable. Pain never left Tim's body for the next 35 years, increasing in intensity and deterioration stages that led to a myriad of complications as the years progressed. What did not deteriorate was Tim's passion to live a life where he chose joy no matter the pain; no matter the cost.

His wife Anastasia wrote: "Tim's faith was lived out and was contagious. He said, 'Choose joy; never, never, never, give up; the rule of the final inch; play to win not to lose; look to the One who designed you and let Him carry you through any circumstance that life hands you as your journey continues. Invite the power of the Holy Spirit...' We were all modeled by his life. Tim's signature book became You Gotta' Keep Dancin' and he taught us how...One always finds inspiring and uplifting messages within Tim's books. Tim's life may have changed with his accident, but he never missed a beat in what his life message was and continued to be; no boundary or limitation exists when God is in control and we allow Him to be. In suffering, we can still choose joy. In chaos, we

> IN SUFFERING, WE CAN STILL CHOOSE JOY. IN CHAOS, WE CAN STILL FIND PEACE.

can still find peace." In his book Tim wrote, "Pain is inevitable, but misery is optional. We cannot avoid pain, but we can avoid joy."

OUR JOY AS CHRISTIANS IS NOT SO MUCH A FEELING AS IT IS OF A CHOICE.

The choice is yours. Our joy as Christians is not so much a feeling as it is of a choice. **1 Thessalonians 5:16** says,

"Be joyful always." GNB

We have to embrace a life of joy. We have to conquer with joy. There is an interesting story about Nathaniel Hawthorne. One day he came home heartbroken, feeling like a failure because he had been fired from his job. His wife made this response: "Now you can write your book!" "What are we going to live on in the meantime?" asked her husband. Then she pulled out a substantial amount of money, and said, "I have always known you were a man of genius. I knew that someday you would write a masterpiece. So every week, out of the money you gave me for housekeeping, I saved a little bit. Here is enough to last us for a whole year." By choosing to embrace her husband's apparent defeat with joy and optimism, the door was opened for him to write one of the greatest novels of American literature, *The Scarlet Letter.*

Joy is a decision. In the words of Dr. Steven C. Riser, "The truth is that no one can do for you what God expects you to do. Joy is a choice! Trusting that, with God, there are no impossible circumstances, enables us to live as victors rather than victims. It's when our future looks the bleakest that our Lord provides the biggest surprises." Paul told the Thessalonians:

THE TRUTH IS THAT NO ONE CAN DO FOR YOU WHAT GOD EXPECTS YOU TO DO. JOY IS A CHOICE!

> **"Thank God no matter what happens. This is the way God wants you who belong to Christ Jesus to live" (1 Thessalonians 5:18 MSG).**

When you live a life of continuous thanksgiving, then you are choosing a lifetime of joy. A lot of people believe that joy is an end result. However, it is a state of being. And the best way to begin to experience joy is to determine to be joyful. It is your life and you have to choose how to live it; choose to be joyful.

EXPRESS THE JOY

> **"A merry heart does good, like medicine, but a broken spirit dries the bones" (Proverbs 17:22 NKJV).**

If ever joy is in your heart it must break out on your face. Joy is a magnet; it is winsome; it is infectious. Is any joyful? Let him sing songs and shout praises in thanksgiving to God. Dale Carnegie, one of the most influential authors of the 19th century who wrote the book, 'How to win Friends and Influence people' said, "The expression you wear on your face is more important than the clothes you wear on your back."

To be truly joyful, we must express it. At times, you see a woman dressed in fine apparel, gold and all kinds of things but a look at her face betrays her inner status. Our face is the mirror of our inner man; the expression we bear is infectious and can affect the people around us. As Christians we have been called to distribute joy everywhere we go

OUR FACE IS THE MIRROR OF OUR INNER MAN.

and what better way to do this than to demonstrate it. If we are going to have joy, then we must express it. William James, American Philosopher wrote, "We don't laugh because we're happy; we're happy because we laugh." It is not enough to be joyful, act joyful. The psalmist declared,

> **"This is the day the LORD has made; we will rejoice and be glad in it" (Psalm 118:24 NKJV).**

Everywhere the Bible talks about joy, it talks about expressing it; in singing, in praises, in worship, in glory. The Bible says 'a cheerful spirit does good as a medicine.' Sometimes we frown, to make a point. We want people to realize how angry we are. But it doesn't make you winsome, it doesn't make you attractive, it doesn't make you loved. In fact, it harms you; not only your physical being, it harms you emotionally and makes you a victim of emotional problems. One psychiatrist was asked: 'How can you help those who are very sad; those who find it very difficult to be happy?' The psychiatrist told them to open the door of their house, come out to the sunshine and give joy to somebody else. When last did a song come to your lips? When last did you sing a song of joy?

IT IS NOT ENOUGH TO BE JOYFUL, ACT JOYFUL.

Paul told the Philippians,

> **"Rejoice in the Lord always. Again I say, Rejoice!" (Philippians 4:4 KJV)**

It is not enough to try to rejoice; force yourself to rejoice. Rejoice, even though there are no things to rejoice about; rejoice in the Lord. While washing dishes, rejoice; while driving, rejoice in the Lord. When young wives meet their husbands, rejoice in the Lord. When old mothers get home, rejoice in the Lord. Moffat's translation says, "By the help of the Lord always keep a glad spirit." There is enough in this world to make us sad. We are faced with a lot of responsibilities and problems, but by the help of the Lord always keep a glad spirit. The wise King Solomon says in **Proverb 15:13,**

> **"A glad heart makes a shining face, but by the sorrow of the heart the spirit is broken." (BBE)**

This is about physical expression, not just spiritual possession. This is external manifestation, not just internal. A cheerful heart makes the face cheerful. If you have it inside you, then let it come out. Express it in joy. The Bible talks about heaven as a place of joy, gladness, happiness and goodness.

Learn to smile, let your voice ring out in laughter. Someone wrote on the power of a smile:

> It costs nothing but creates much.
>
> It enriches those who receive, without impoverishing those who give.
>
> It happens in a flash and the memory of it lasts forever
>
> None are so rich they can get along without it and none so poor but are richer for its benefits.
>
> It creates happiness in the home, fosters good will in business and is the countersign of friends.
>
> It is rest to the weary, daylight to the discouraged, sunshine to the sad and Nature's best antidote for trouble.

Joyful people know how to smile. Imagine the immense effect of your smile on another person. Smiling makes you welcoming. It makes others feel comfortable around you and it is infectious. It lights up a dark room. There is a popular aphorism that it takes more muscles to frown than to smile; that frowning exerts more energy than smiling. Though this homespun wisdom might not be totally true as proved by anatomists, the moral is that our efforts will be better expended on making ourselves pleasant company for others than going through life as gloomy beings. Why frown when you can easily smile?

Much more than that, the life of joyful people bubbles over in laughter. Joy is very difficult to hide; it has to be expressed. God wants our lives to be full of joy and laughter. In **Isaiah 51:3**, He promised,

> **"Likewise I, GOD, will comfort Zion, comfort all her mounds of ruins. I'll transform her dead ground into Eden, her moonscape into the garden of GOD, A place filled with exuberance and laughter, thankful voices and melodic songs" (MSG).**

In **Jeremiah 30:19**, He says,

> **"Thanksgivings will pour out of the windows;**

laughter will spill through the doors. Things will get better and better. Depression days are over. They'll thrive, they'll flourish. The days of contempt will be over" (MSG).

Laughter is an audible expression of an inward feeling of joy. As we rejoice in the Lord, he wants laughter to spill through our doors; the sounds of rejoicing to burst forth from our tents. Laughter is the essential behaviour of a happy joyful person. It allows us to be more spontaneous, let go of defensiveness; release inhibitions and express our true feelings. When laughter is shared, it binds people together and increases intimacy. Victor Borge, U.S entertainer and pianist, said, "Laughter is the shortest distance between two people." Much more, laughter is good for our health, as modern research has shown that it boosts our immunity, lowers stress, relaxes our muscles, lowers blood

LAUGHTER IS AN AUDIBLE EXPRESSION OF AN INWARD FEELING OF JOY.

pressure and prevents heart disease.

True laughter that results from a joyful heart is Spirit-born. Someone commented, "True laughter is true prayer. When you laugh, the whole nature laughs with you. It echoes and resounds and makes life worthwhile. When things go right, everybody can laugh but when everything falls apart, and yet you laugh, that is evolution and growth. Nothing in life is more worthy than your laughter." True laughter wells from deep within; it occurs spontaneously without a reason. It exhibits the joy of the Lord.

GIVE THANKS IN EVERYTHING

"Let us come before his presence with thanksgiving, and make a joyful noise unto him with psalms" (Psalm 95:2 KJV).

It has been said, "Some people count their blessings while others add up their sorrow." When you come in contact with people who do not give thanks, they relate to you, in chronological order, the sorrow they have gone through. I always encourage people to take all things with a heart of gratitude, not for granted. We can only maintain our joy if we give thanks in everything. We are to give thanks, not for everything but in everything. He who forgets the language of gratitude can never be on speaking terms with happiness.

WE ARE TO GIVE THANKS, NOT FOR EVERYTHING BUT IN EVERYTHING.

Joy is sometimes punctured by an ungrateful heart. Someone commented, "Happiness comes when we stop wailing about the troubles we have and offer thanks for all the troubles we do not have. The secret of happiness and success is not doing what you like but liking what you do. Those who grumble are never happy, but those who are grateful find joy in the midst of their circumstances." We must pause to give thanks for what people have done for us. Let's not keep listing our problems. Be appreciative, be thankful. When you appreciate people for what they had done in the past, they tend to do more.

It has been said, "Thankfulness is the secret of joy."

HE WHO FORGETS THE LANGUAGE OF GRATITUDE CAN NEVER BE ON SPEAKING TERMS WITH HAPPINESS.

Give thanks to God in everything. Thank Him for the things He has done for you. Thank Him for the things He is giving you. Be thankful. Sometimes we may find ourselves in certain conditions we do not expect; but what can we do about it? Learn to like what you do because you know that there is a joy ahead of you.

BE AN EVANGELIST OF JOY

> **"Grief can take care of itself, but to get the full value of joy you must have somebody to divide it with." Mark Twain**

Give others the joy that you have. Be an apostle of joy. Apostle was derived from *'apostilo'* which means 'sent out.' The apostles shared the gospel, they told others about the good news and they shared joyful choruses. Be someone that gives joy to somebody else. Make it happen for others. The Bible says,

> **"They that sow in tears shall reap in joy" (Psalm 126:5).**

Ralph Waldo Emerson, American essayist and poet said, "Scatter Joy." Make it happen for others, and it will happen for you. Find someone who is hurting and help him or her. Spread the wings of joy. Don't be too self involved as to ignore the pain of others. Karl Menninger, notable American Psychiatrist wrote, "One of the secret of unhappiness is to keep pursuing happiness for yourself. Give it away; it multiplies." Give it out. Sow the seeds of joy. Serve and help others.

FIND SOMEONE WHO IS HURTING AND HELP HIM OR HER. SPREAD THE WINGS OF JOY.

This is something about life; those who will be

joyful are those who are ready to sow. One big way in which you can be an evangelist of joy is by witnessing. Proverb 11:38 says,

> **"The fruit of the righteous is a tree of life. He who is wise wins souls" (WEB).**

The Bible says about the apostles of Jesus Christ that when they went out, they came back rejoicing. Many Christians are not joyful because they are self-centered; they have turned Christianity to an 'ostrich' religion rather than an outreach. People have equaled spiritual prosperity to material prosperity. God promised material possessions but gives joy beyond what money can buy. The world doesn't want to know how many great things you have. The question they want to ask you is: What is my take on this? So go out and witness to somebody; go and share the Word of God.

Be an evangelist of joy. Frederick Wm. Faber, English hymn writer and Oratorian, wrote, "There are souls in this world which have the gift of finding joy everywhere and of leaving it behind them when they go." Be that person. Let people rejoice because you came around and leave joy with them when you leave.

GIVE IT ENTIRELY TO GOD

> **"Never worry about anything, but in every situation let your petitions be made known to God in prayers and requests, with thanksgiving. Then God's peace, which goes far beyond anything we can imagine, will guard your hearts and minds in Christ Jesus" (Philippians 4:6 ISV).**

Sometimes we are not joyful because we have not given everything to God. We give God the main points, but we want to perform the subsidiary points. We give God the driver seat yet we want to drive the car. We want God to take our picture yet we stand behind the camera. Life does not work that way. We must give it entirely to God.

There are certain issues we cannot solve; certain

people we cannot change. Someone said, "The secret of happiness is to accept the impossible, do without the indispensable and bear with the intolerant." To which I add, "Pray when it is inevitable."

In relating with people, I have discovered that there are certain people we cannot please. It doesn't matter what you do; you cannot please them. There are certain bosses who just hate us. No matter how hard we try to make the situation right, they still continue to make things difficult for us. In situations like this when we face issues that will make us sad, we must learn to commit everything to God, in order to regain our joy. We must learn to pray, to ask, to seek and to knock at God's door on such occasions. We have to give it to God.

Have you learned to pray? Have you learned to entirely hand it over to God? Some issues go beyond physical persuasion to produce results. A son or daughter that is not doing well; an employee that does not take to instruction, or a person who gives you agony and sadness in your soul. All efforts to stimulate change meets with stiff resistance; then you know you have to commit it to God. Man's extremity gives room for God's opportunity. Sometimes we feel we must do things ourselves, but God wants us to look up to him. He wants to handle it; he wants us to ask Him for help. Jesus says in John 16:24,

MAN'S EXTREMITY GIVES ROOM FOR GOD'S OPPORTUNITY.

> **"Hitherto have ye asked nothing in my name: ask, and ye shall receive, that your joy may be full" (KJV).**

James 4:2 tells us,

> **"Ye lust, and have not: ye kill, and desire to have, and cannot obtain: ye fight and war, yet ye have not, because ye ask not."**

Ask that your joy might be full. Why not pray about it? Don't engage in physical strive, don't quarrel about it; hand it over to God. The Psalmist says in **Psalms 40:1-3,**

> **"I waited patiently for the LORD; and he inclined unto me, and heard my cry. He brought me up also out of an horrible pit, out of the miry clay, and set my feet upon a rock, and established my goings. And he hath put a new song in my mouth, even praise unto our God: many shall see it, and fear, and shall trust in the LORD."**

What did the Psalmist do? He did not discuss it with anybody. Rather he told God about it, he committed it to God. If you discuss it, you will be disgusted. If you fume, you will be frustrated. If you fret, you will get depressed. If you fight, you become a fool. Let out the steam but give it to God. He only can stand the heat. Paul told the Philippians:

> **"Be careful for nothing; but in everything by prayer and supplication with thanksgiving let**

your requests be made known unto God. And the peace of God, which passeth all understanding, shall keep your hearts and minds through Christ Jesus" (Philippians 4:6 KJV).

The Message Bible translates:

"Don't fret or worry. Instead of worrying, pray. Let petitions and praises shape your worries into prayers, letting God know your concerns. Before you know it, a sense of God's wholeness, everything coming together for good, will come and settle you down. It's wonderful what happens when Christ displaces worry at the center of your life" (Philippians 4:6).

Don't allow situations to disturb your mind. In spite of the situations around you; God will guard your heart and your mind in Christ Jesus. When people gossip and say evil things about you, guard your heart. When men rise up against you, seek the Lord as your ultimate defense. Commit yourself to prayer. When all around you is trouble, seek the peace and joy of the Lord.

The Bible tells the story of Ahithophel, the chief adviser to King David. Ahithophel was a man of great wisdom. It was said that his counseling was as important as that of the angels of God. King David was a man who also had great wisdom and many people wanted to sit and listen to him. When David worships God, he expresses joy, and God gives him a revelation. But in spite of his profound wisdom, David still needed the counsel of Ahithophel to make decisions. There came a time in the life of David when his son Absalom rebelled against him, and David was exiled. Many of his friends made a mockery of him but what hurt David most was the fact that Ahithophel joined the conspiracy. Imagine one of your best friends, the person who knows how you think, who knows your ways, your life, your secrets; who knows everything about you joining a conspiracy against you. That is what Satan does.

When he wants to attack, he uses the closest person to you.

David could have gotten bitter; he could have fought with Ahithophel; rather he chose to commit it to God. Sometimes you know the battle is not in the physical, natural or carnal realm; you need to take it to God. **2 Samuel 15:31-32** says,

> **"And one told David, saying, Ahithophel is among the conspirators with Absalom. And David said, O LORD, I pray thee, turn the counsel of Ahithophel into foolishness. And it came to pass, that when David was come to the top of the mount, where he worshipped God..." (KJV)**

David said a very simple prayer, 'Oh Lord, I pray thee turn the counsel of Ahithophel to foolishness.' Good News Bible says,

> **"Please, LORD, turn Ahithophel's advice into nonsense!"**

Contemporary English Version says,

"Please, LORD, keep Ahithophel's plans from working!"

The Message Bible translates,

"Oh, GOD--turn Ahithophel's counsel to foolishness."

Are you going to fume when somebody is against you? Are you going to fight back when somebody is fighting you? Are you going to lose your joy over the issue? Explore prayer and regain your joy. Look at what David did after the prayer.

"And it came to pass, that when David was come to the top of the mount, where he worshipped God."

That is the mystery of it all. These two actions are not coincidental, David prayed and he worshipped on the mountain of the Lord. He came to the summit where God was worshipped. In difficult situations, do not lose your joy; go to the summit to seek the face of God. When you are perplexed, rise up to seek God on His mountain. When Judas joined the conspiracy, what did Jesus do? He went to Gethsemane to cry unto the Lord and the angels ministered to Him.

2 Samuel 17:4 revealed how God defended David and discountenanced the wisdom of Ahithophel.

> **"And Absalom and all the men of Israel said, The counsel of Hushai the Archite is better than the counsel of Ahithophel. For the LORD had appointed to defeat the good counsel of Ahithophel, to the intent that the LORD might bring evil upon Absalom" (KJV).**

The counsel of Ahithophel was obviously a good counsel but God nullified his counsel that he might defend his servant David. There are many people who are giving wise counsels against you, but the Lord will defeat such counsel that you may retain your joy. The Psalmist cried,

"Hear my cry, O God; attend unto my prayer. From the end of the earth will I cry unto thee, when my heart is overwhelmed: lead me to the rock that is higher than I" (Psalm 61:1-2 KJV).

David was like a man who was about to sink, he was overwhelmed by the waves; he could no longer fight the situation, yet at the last moment he sees a rock in the midst of the sea and he cries out, 'lead me to the rock that is higher than I.' Hand over your case to God. Give God room to act on your behalf. That is the only way you can move from weeping to joy, from grumbling to gratitude, from perplexity to peace. That is the only way you can move from reciting the chronicles of your troubles to talking about the good news of your triumph. That is the only way to have joy in the present and faith in a glorious future.

S I X

ENTERING INTO THE FULNESS OF JOY

"Real joy comes not from ease or riches or from the praise of men, but from doing something worthwhile."
Wilfred T. Grenfell

THE JOY OF SALVATION

S alvation and joy are mutually inclusive. To fully experience true joy, we must be saved. When we repent and accept Jesus Christ as our Lord and Saviour, we become new beings. The realization that our sins are forgiven and that God welcomes us is first met by surprise, then a pure joy. Like C. S. Lewis, we are *Surprised by Joy*. It sure feels good to be saved and free from all entanglements.

The Psalmist says,

> "My soul shall be joyful in the LORD; it shall rejoice in His salvation" (Psalm 35:9).

In **Psalm 9:14**, he says,

> "I will rejoice in thy salvation."

And **Psalm 118:14** says,

> "For the LORD, is my strength and song; He also has become my salvation."

The Prophet Isaiah wrote:

> "Therefore with joy you will draw water from the wells of salvation" (Isaiah 12:3).

And he said in **Isaiah 35:10**,

> "And the ransomed of the LORD shall return, and come to Zion with songs and everlasting joy upon their heads: they shall obtain joy and gladness, and sorrow and sighing shall flee away."

The salvation package contains resounding joy; with salvation comes the indwelling Spirit of God and the fruit of His Spirit is Joy. There is no convincing power in a gloomy Christian; let the joy

THE SALVATION PACKAGE CONTAINS RESOUNDING JOY.

of the Lord shine through you. It has been said, "To be filled with God is to be filled with joy." Ronald Newhouse said, "There's nothing more contradictory than an unenthusiastic Christian. The Bible tells us that God loves us so much, in fact, that God gave his only son so that all who believe in him will have everlasting life. Nothing, not even death, can separate us from God's love! If we really believe that, we can't help but overflow with joy!" Salvation fills our hearts to overflowing with the joy of the Lord.

THE JOY OF FAITHFULNESS

True joy comes after faithfully serving the Lord and serving our fellow men. Joy is the by-product of

FAITHFULNESS IS DAILY CONSTANCY, LOYALTY AND UNYIELDING OBEDIENCE, IN THE PURSUIT OF WHAT GOD HAS CALLED US TO DO.

service. To enter into the joy of the Lord, we must be faithful in using the talents and gifts given us to further the cause of the gospel.

Faithfulness is daily constancy, loyalty and unyielding obedience, in the pursuit of what God has called us to do. God expects us to be true to the cause he has committed into our hands and to do it with singularity of purpose. In the successful accomplishment of this task, lies our joy and reward. Jesus told the parable of the servants that received certain talents from their master in Matthew 25. The one that received five talents put it to good use and gained five more. The one that received two talents also maximized it and got two more but the one who got one talent buried it for safekeeping and did not invest it into any worthwhile pursuit. Let's hear the judgement of the master:

"So he who had received five talents came and brought five other talents, saying, 'Lord, you delivered to me five talents; look, I have gained five more talents besides them. His lord said to him, 'Well done, good and faithful servant; you were faithful over a few things, I will make you ruler over many things. Enter into the joy of your lord. He also who had received two talents came and said, 'Lord, you delivered to me two talents; look, I have gained two more talents besides them.'"His lord said to him, 'Well done, good and faithful servant; you have been faithful over a few things, I will make you ruler over many things. Enter into the joy of your lord.'"Then he who had received the one talent came and said, 'Lord, I knew you to be a hard man, reaping where you have not sown, and gathering where you have not scattered seed.' And I was afraid, and went and hid your talent in the ground. Look, there you have what is yours.'"But his lord answered and said to him, 'You wicked and lazy servant, you knew that I reap where I have not sown, and gather where I have not scattered seed... Therefore take the talent from him, and give it to him who has ten talents. 'For to everyone who has, more will be given, and he will have abundance; but from him who does not have, even what he has will be taken away. 'And cast the unprofitable servant into the outer darkness. There will be weeping and gnashing of teeth." (Matthew 25:20-26, 28-30 NKJV)

WHEN WE DO HIS WILL AND WORK HIS WAY, WE WILL EXPERIENCE HIS JOY.

Enter into the joy of your Lord! When we do His will and work His way, we will experience His joy. Nothing gives the believer so much joy as furthering the cause of the Master; preaching the word, witnessing to Christ and bringing souls to the Kingdom. The Lord promised,

"He who goes out weeping, carrying seed for sowing, Will assuredly come again with joy, carrying his sheaves" (Psalm 126:6 WEB).

When we sow our time and resources into the Kingdom, we will undoubtedly reap the harvest of joy. Paul and Silas, while in chains experienced continuous joy despite all, and this brought victory for them. **Acts 16:25-26** says,

> **"And at midnight Paul and Silas prayed, and sang praises unto God: and the prisoners heard them. And suddenly there was a great earthquake, so that the foundations of the prison were shaken: and immediately all the doors were opened, and every one's bands were loosed."**

However, our ultimate joy lies in fellowship with the Father. There is joy in utilizing God's gifts and doing God's works but we find greater joy when we have a relationship with Him. He is the eternal source of joy and when we are in Him, we continually draw from this well-spring. Charles H. Spurgeon, eighteenth century preacher, wrote, "Nothing gives the believer so much joy as fellowship with Christ...If you know anything of the inner life, you will confess that our highest, purest and most enduring joys must be the fruit of the tree of life which is in the midst of the Paradise of God. The joy of the Lord is solid and enduring. Vanity hath not looked upon it, but discretion and prudence testify that it abideth the test of years, and is in time and in eternity worthy to be called 'the only true delight.' For nourishment, consolation, exhilaration and refreshment, no wine can rival the love of Jesus."

The joy we experience in relating with God is continuous and this joy will become complete when we get to heaven; when we "receive the crown of glory that doesn't fade away" **(1 Peter 5:4 WEB).**

THE JOY OF SOUL-WINNING

Unparalleled joy is experienced when we evangelize and win a soul into the Kingdom of God. Soul winning produces universal joy; the joy of the soul winner, the converted sinner; the Saviour and the angels. The Bible tells us that the Heaven resounds with great joy and there is rejoicing among the angels when sinners repent.

> "Suppose one of you had a hundred sheep and lost one. Wouldn't you leave the ninety-nine in the wilderness and go after the lost one until you found it? When found, you can be sure you would put it across your shoulders, rejoicing, and when you got home call in your friends and neighbors, saying, 'Celebrate with me! I've found my lost sheep!' Count on it--there's more joy in heaven over one sinner's rescued life than over ninety-nine good people in no need of rescue. Or imagine a woman who has ten coins and loses one. Won't she light a lamp and scour the house, looking in every nook and cranny until she finds it? And when she finds it you can be sure she'll call her friends and neighbors: 'Celebrate with me! I found my lost coin!' Count on it--that's the kind of party God's angels throw every time one lost soul turns to God" (Luke 15:4-10 MSG).

God places a very high value on our souls. He prices us greatly and desires that no human be lost. In **Matthew 16:26**, He asked,

> **"For what is a man profited, if he shall gain the whole world, and lose his own soul? Or what shall a man give in exchange for his soul?"**

THERE IS NO GREATER THING THAT GLORIFIES GOD AND BRINGS JOY THAN WINNING ONE SOUL FOR WHICH CHRIST DIED.

The soul winner experiences great joy because he values what the master values and brings great glory to God. There is no greater thing that glorifies God and brings joy than winning one soul for which Christ died. Have you lost your joy? Then tell someone about Jesus. Be a witness to Christ. Commit yourself to the great commission and as lives are changed, you will experience unfathomable joy. The Bible encourages soul winning. **Proverbs 11:30** says,

"The fruit of the righteous is a tree of life, and he who wins souls is wise."

We may pray for the lost, provide for their needs, motivate them but nothing compares to winning them to Christ. Harriet Beecher said, "The greatest thing that one human being can do for another human being is to win them to Jesus." Soul winning demonstrates the love of God and its fruits reflect His Joy. Someone said, "The bringing of a person to Jesus is the highest achievement in this life."

If we truly believe that souls that have not accepted Christ are headed for an eternity of hell fire, anguish and pain, then we should do all in our power to persuade them to turn from sin to Jesus Christ. James told the apostles,

> **"You may be sure that whoever brings a sinner back from his wrong path will save his soul from death and cover a multitude of sins" (James 5:20 ISV).**

In the words of Charles H. Spurgeon, "If I were utterly selfish and had no care for anything but my own happiness, I would choose, if I might under God, to be a soul winner, for never did I know perfect overflowing, unutterable happiness of the purest and most ennobling order, till I first heard of one who had sought and found the Saviour through my means." Our wells of joy fill up and bubble over, when we win souls to Christ.

> "For you yourselves know, brethren, that our coming to you was not in vain. But even after we had suffered before and were spitefully treated at Philippi, as you know, we were bold in our God to speak to you the gospel of God in much conflict... For this reason we also thank God without ceasing, because when you received the word of God which you heard from us, you welcomed it not as the word of men, but as it is in truth, the word of God, which also effectively works in you who believe... For what is our hope, or joy, or

crown of rejoicing? Is it not even you in the presence of our Lord Jesus Christ at His coming? For you are our glory and joy" (1 Thessalonians 2:1-2, 19-20 NKJV).

THE JOY OF SERVICE

Joy also comes when we live our lives in service towards others; when we aspire to improve and bring joy to the lives of people. Are you sad, go out and give joy to others and you will regain your joy. There is joy in reaching out to the weak, consoling the downcast, encouraging the dispirited and ministering to the sick. True joy lies in giving. Are you joyful? Share it. A Swedish proverb says, "Shared joy is double joy; shared sorrow is half a sorrow."

TRUE JOY LIES IN GIVING. ARE YOU JOYFUL? SHARE IT.

Be committed to a noble cause. Give of yourself to humanity. Don't be wrapped up in yourself. George

Bernard Shaw, prolific playwright, wrote, "This is the true joy in life...being used for a purpose recognized by yourself as a mighty one... being a force of Nature instead of a feverish selfish little clod of ailments and grievances complaining that the world will not devote itself to making you happy."

The joy of life is using it for something significant. Someone wrote, "The joy of life is living it and doing things of worth, in making bright and fruitful all the barren spots of the earth; ...for only he knows perfect joy, whose little bit of soil is richer ground than what it was when he began to toil."

RESTORATION OF JOY

Though we might have sinned, experienced failure, had bad experiences and gone through difficult times, God can restore our joy. Joy can be renewed; the covenant of joy can be daily reenacted. Your joy can be revitalized. The Lord promised,

"Be glad then, ye children of Zion, and rejoice in the LORD your God: for he hath given you the former rain moderately, and he will cause to come down for you the rain, the former rain, and the latter rain in the first month. And the floors shall be full of wheat, and the fats shall overflow with wine and oil. And I will restore to you the years that the locust hath eaten, the cankerworm, and the caterpillar, and the palmerworm, my great army which I sent among you. And ye shall eat in plenty, and be satisfied, and praise the name of the LORD your God that hath dealt wondrously with you: and my people shall never be ashamed" (Joel 2:23-26).

God will restore your joy. The Lord declared,

"You shall no longer be termed Forsaken, nor shall your land any more be termed Desolate; But you shall be called Hephzibah, and your land Beulah; For the LORD delights in you, and your land shall be married" (Isaiah 62:4).

Learn to cast all your cares on him. Develop an

intimacy with Him. Explore the vast possibilities inherent in prayer. Prayer is a form of catharsis; where we empty our bitterness and receive joy. To live a life full of joy:

Break away from the power of resentment. Choose to forgive.

Don't replay bitter experiences; you will suffer more from it.

Accept and adapt to people; don't try to change them.

Don't win an argument, win souls.

Don't be frank, be fair.

Don't analyze, appreciate.

Don't put labels and don't read minds.

Don't insinuate. If you do, you will not be joyful.

Don't rewind sad memories; tune in to joyful ones.

Be a child again. When a child comes to a puddle, he jumps in and plays in it; when old men see puddles, they grumble and avoid it. Learn to appreciate life's puddles.

Have no racial prejudice or personal bias. Love like Christ.

Do not go looking for information that will not be useful. Too much information can deform you. Stop the flow of gossip and slander.

Use knowledge productively to make yourself happy; not something to make you sad.

Maintain your innocence; it preserves your joy.

If you have lost your salvation, confront, do not conceal it; don't compromise, confess and your joy will be restored.

Just enjoy life.

Life is too short to be used in nursing bitterness or entertaining unhappiness. Learn to enjoy life. Be joyful; embrace joy. Let the joy of the Lord radiate from you. Be the sunshine that lights the gloom. Bring joy to your world.

EPILOGUE

Living a life of joy is a wonderful experience. But it's a life better experienced in Christ Jesus. You can give your life to Christ today. Please join me in this prayer;

> **Dear Lord, I confess my sins to you. I accept you as my Lord and Saviour. Forgive my sins and bring me into oneness with you. Fill me with the joy of salvation. Let your glory shine forth in my life. Help me to live in continuous joy despite life's circumstances and to share your joy with those around me. I ask all these in Jesus name, Amen.**

I believe this book has made a great impact
in your life. You can share your experience
with me.

Please write:

Rev. Prof. G. E. Erhabor P.
O. Box 1154, Ile-Ife
gregerhabor7@yahoo.com
www.spokesmancom.org

FROM WORRY TO WELL-BEING

The quality of our lives will be determined by how we handle worry. Worry has been described as the mother of all diseases. However, we can overcome this habit. Regardless of the nature of your worry or how long you have indulged this habit, you can take a definite step to freedom today.

This book will teach you how to live your life free of worry and enjoy every moment of your existence here on earth.

SEIZE YOUR DAY; CONTROL YOUR DESTINY

The best way to invent the future is to purposefully channel everyday. When we make the best of today, we make the best of life.

This book will teach you how to harness and effectively utilize the potentials inherent in your mornings.

REVISED EDITION

YOUR TIME IN YOUR HAND

———— ❖ ————

The quality of our lives will be largely determined by how we manage our time.

Greatness comes as a result of effective planning, diligent work and most especially, brilliancy in managing time.

This is a must-read for everyone who wants to maximize every moment and leave an indelible mark for generations to come.

REVISED EDITION

THE SEVEN MOST EFFECTIVE AFFIRMATIONS TOWARDS ACHIEVING YOUR GOALS

Biblically, affirmations are proclamations of faith. They are declarations that determine our destiny and pilot our lives. The Seven Affirmations are simple statements that would help us live a productive life and fulfill our purpose.

It is handy for all occasions.

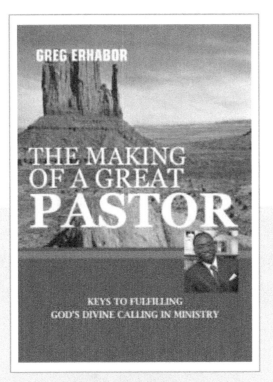

THE MAKING
OF A GREAT PASTOR

Great pastors are those who leave a long-lasting legacy behind. They do not only build institutions, they build men. They have an excellent spirit. To them being called to serve, is a privilege, not a right. These pastors do not emphasize what men owe them but see themselves as being called to serve.

Looking for a book that will ignite your passion for ministry and give you added impetus to serve God and build men in your local church? This is the book for you. It is filled with practical principles on how you can build your life, build men under your care and leave a long-lasting legacy behind.

OTHER BOOKS
BY THE AUTHOR

———— ❖ ————

DARE TO FULFILL
YOUR DESTINY

Everyone who reads this book, regardless of his present status,
age or calling can discover in it practical steps on how to
maximize his life and turn momentary set backs into monumental
opportunities.

101 QUOTABLE
QUOTES ON PRAYER-
APPLES OF GOLD

Effective prayer depends on a good understanding of the
subject. This book serves as a quick resource material on the
subject of prayer.

COMMITMENT: THE HALLMARK OF GREATNESS

This book addresses the question: 'What will I do to change my generation? And not 'What can I get from my generation? It will teach you how to move from mere interest to commitment to a noble cause, mission or institution. It will teach you how you can leave your footprints on the sands of time and move your generation forward towards positive and long-lasting achievement.

IT PAYS TO FORGIVE

An ounce of forgiveness is worth several pounds of medicine. Forgiveness is the greatest therapeutic agent to keep your head, heart and stomach from the physician's medication and the surgeon's scalpel. It really pays to forgive. This book will tell you how and why you must make forgiveness a lifestyle and begin to swim in the ocean of inner serenity. It is a book that will surely turn your destiny around.

GOD CENTERED
PROSPERITY

Prosperity is not the right of an exclusive club. God designed that we all prosper in all we do. Biblical prosperity comes when we come to terms with the principles laid down by God in His word. This book will help you attain to true prosperity without compromising your principles. You too can be prosperous and holy.

MAKING YOUR
LIFE COUNT

We all have the ability to impact our generation and make our lives count. This book will help you rise above the drudgery of everyday living and put a touch of nobility in all you do.

THE TEST, TRAVAILS AND TRIUMPH OF LEADERSHIP

This contemporary insight into the life of Gideon and his men will teach you the principles of becoming the great leader you desire to be. It will also help you develop the abilities required to surmount obstacles and establish God's purpose in your life and the lives of those God has called you to lead.

It is a book for all leaders in all walks of life; both in spiritual and secular callings. You can be the Gideon of today to give the inspired leadership to your generation.

SEEDS OF EXCELLENCE

Excellence is an ever increasing quest! It can be practised by everybody. This book will inspire you to aspire to something beyond the ordinary. It will lift you up from the quick sand of mediocrity to the solid rock of excellence and greatness.